# BOBCAT

Weekly Reader Books presents

# BOBCAT

## Virginia F. Voight

*Illustrated by Lloyd Bloom*

DODD, MEAD & COMPANY

*New York*

This book is a presentation of
**Weekly Reader Books.**

Weekly Reader Books offers
book clubs for children from
preschool through junior high school.
All quality hardcover books are selected by
a distinguished Weekly Reader Selection Board.

For further information write to:
**Weekly Reader Books**
1250 Fairwood Ave.
Columbus, Ohio 43216

Library of Congress Cataloging in Publication Data

Voight, Virginia Frances.
Bobcat.

SUMMARY: Follows the experiences of a bobcat
in his first year of life.
1. Bobcat—Legends and stories.  [1.  Bobcat—
Fiction]  I.  Bloom, Lloyd.  II.  Title.
PZ10.3.V9Bo    [Fic]    77–16876
ISBN 0–396–07538–X

*To my friend Bill Massey*

# CONTENTS

# 1. The Bobcat Den

IT WAS A sunny April morning in the north woods. The sky was the color of a bluejay's wing. The air was cool and nippy, but the sun shone bright and warm. A few sunbeams stole down through the branches of the pines and hemlocks to peek into the den on Juniper Hill. The den, a small cave opening on a rock ledge, was the home of a mother bobcat and her two kittens.

The kittens were tiny creatures only nine days old. Their short legs were too weak to hold them up. Their ears lay so flat on their heads that they scarcely looked like ears at all. Until now, their eyes had been tightly closed, but this morning something exciting had happened. Their eyes were open!

Not that they could see much, as yet. Stub Tail, the largest of the little cats, could make out only a hazy golden glow at the entrance to the den. He started to crawl toward it, but his mother caught him by the loose skin at the back of his neck and dropped him gently down beside his sister.

Stub Tail suddenly remembered breakfast. He shoved his

sister aside and pressed his face against his mother and nursed greedily. As the rich, warm milk flowed into his stomach, he forgot about the light. Bulging with milk, he cuddled close to his mother and purred a contented song as he fell asleep.

Until now, the kittens had wanted only to drink milk and sleep. But after their eyes opened, they grew stronger and more lively every day. Stub Tail liked to pounce on his sister with fierce little growls and pretend to bite and scratch. He was bigger and stronger than she, but she always fought back with spirit as they scuffled and rolled about in mock battles. If their mother thought that the game was getting too rough, she would cuff them apart with her soft paws. Then the kittens would jump on her and climb all over her, biting her ears, nibbling at her cheeks, and mauling her short tail.

The mother cat always kept the den and the kittens clean. At least once a day she would hold each kitten down with her paw and use her rough tongue to wash it from head to foot. Soon the kittens learned the habit of being neat, and they would wash their own faces with their little paws.

Stub Tail and his sister were always hungry, and their mother had to hunt often to keep up her supply of milk. While the kittens were tiny, she left the den only after dark. Before she set out, she made sure that the little ones were curled up on their bed of leaves and moss.

As soon as she had caught a rabbit, or enough mice to make a meal, she would hurry home. Other predators were on the prowl in the forest, and there was always a chance that one might find the den and kill her kittens.

In the daytime, while their mother rested, the kittens would crouch at the entrance to the den. Their eyes, grown strong now, sparkled with wonder as they stared at the unknown world outside their home.

When a breeze stirred the branches of the evergreens, sunbeams seemed to dance on the rock ledge. One morning Stub Tail started outside to try to catch one of the bright things. A sharp cry from his mother called him back. He was still too little to venture outside the den. Stub Tail obeyed her but he whimpered in protest. More and more the outside world was calling to him. His whiskers quivered with excitement when he saw a bird fly past the den. His ears pricked up when the petals of pine cones fell softly from somewhere above. He could not see the red squirrel in a tree that shaded the ledge, pulling cones apart to get at the seeds. The squirrel

scolded loudly if a bluejay flew near, and the jay would
scream back at him. Stub Tail longed to know what was making the sounds, but he dared not venture outside to look.

One day a strange wild cry came from the forest. Seconds
later, a handsome bobtailed cat bounded onto the ledge. He

was larger than Stub Tail's mother, and he was carrying a big rabbit in his jaws. He laid the rabbit down and peered into the den. The kittens spat and shrank back. They did not know that the big cat, with his blazing eyes and wide-spreading whiskers, was their father.

The mother bobcat gave a yell and burst from the den. She slammed into her mate and raked his face with her claws. The larger cat shrieked in protest and tried to defend himself, but she was all over him. Finally he turned tail and jumped off the ledge and bounded away into the trees.

The kittens were huddled together at the back of the den, trembling with fright. Now they ran to rub against their mother and reach up to pat her cheeks with their paws. Their mother calmly settled down to eat the rabbit. She would accept gifts of food from her mate, but while the kittens were small, she would not permit him to come near them.

## 2. Danger from the Air

THE APRIL MOON had waned and now it was May. The Indians, who had owned this country long before Stub Tail was born, called May the Planting Moon. They had planted corn in the rich soil beside the pond at the foot of Juniper Hill. Now the Indians were gone. The family, who lived on the farm at the foot of the pond, no longer used the field, and the forest was taking it over again.

Little pines were growing up among the long grasses and wild flowers. There were mats of lowbush blueberries, where foxes, bears, and birds loved to feed. Tangles of raspberries offered shelter and food to rabbits, and clumps of white birch trees gleamed in the sunlight.

Mice and woodchucks lived in the old field. Deer came there at dawn or dusk to feed and to drink from the pond. Stub Tail's mother found the field a good hunting ground close to her den.

Stub Tail was a month old. He was cute and fat and full

of play and high spirits. His fluffy red-brown coat was peppered with black spots. His ears stood up at last, as a cat's ears should. At their tips, tiny tufts of fur gave him a jaunty look. His funny little tail was barred with black, but the underside was white at the tip. His yellow eyes, round as twin moons, sparkled with intelligence. His sister was smaller than him, but otherwise they looked alike.

The mother bobcat sometimes hunted in the daytime now. While she was away, the kittens played on the shady ledge. They could not wander off because they were still too small to climb down the rocks. When their mother was away after dark, they stayed in the den.

Sometimes in the evening, a deep bird cry, that held a note of terror, boomed through the woodland. *Hoo, hoo, hoo-hoo-hooooo.* It was the hunting call of the great horned owl. When Stub Tail's mother heard it, her lip would lift in a snarl that showed her long white fangs. If the family was outside, she would hastily herd the kittens into the den. In this way she made them understand that the bird that made the sound was dangerous to little bobcats.

One day Stub Tail's mother came home with a dead mouse dangling from her mouth. She laid it on the ledge and sat down to see what the kittens would do. They were still dependent on her for milk, but it was time she started to train them to eat meat.

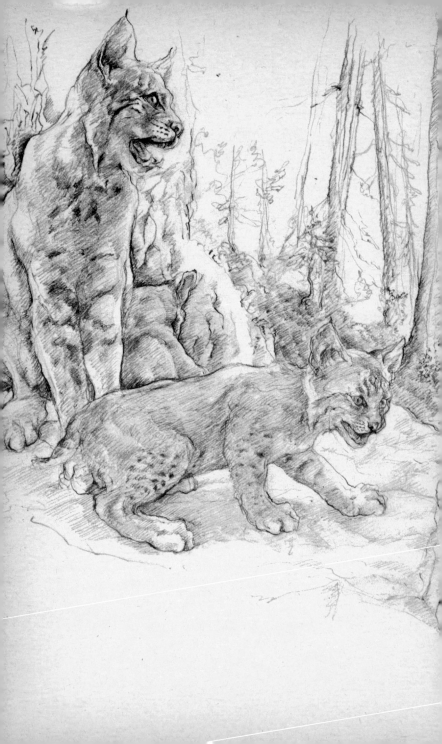

Stub Tail and his sister were both startled and excited by the strange creature. Their little tails twitched nervously. Stub Tail put out a paw and timidly touched the mouse. When he patted the still-warm body, a queer thrill went through him.

He began to bat the mouse about and toss it into the air, in the way that he played with pine cones that fell onto the ledge. His sister got into the game and tried to take the mouse away. Stub Tail held it by one leg and galloped wildly about the ledge. His sister ran after him, and they got into a rough-and-tumble fight. The little female was chewing on Stub Tail's ear when their mother made a soft purry sound which meant "supper." She let go of the ear and ran to her mother. Stub Tail was left with the mouse. He crouched over it and licked it.

During the tug-of-war, the mouse had been torn by little needle-sharp teeth and claws. Stub Tail tasted blood on his tongue. It was not as good as his mother's milk, but there was something about it that sent a tingle through him. His eyes flared green for a moment. Then suddenly he felt very hungry. He ran to his mother and forgot about the mouse.

On another night the bobcat mother brought home a dead rabbit. She tore it open and began to eat. Stub Tail crowded close and tore off a piece of rabbit meat. His first taste of meat made him hungry for more. After that, the mother cat brought home some kind of meat every day.

One night the mother cat carried home a big live bullfrog that she had caught in the pond. This was to be the kittens' first lesson in catching an animal.

She laid the frog down before her wondering kittens. It gave a hoarse croak and hopped frantically away. Sight of the moving creature made Stub Tail's blood race with excitement. He pounced on the frog and clamped down with his claws, but the frog was so big that he could not hold it. It hopped away. Stub Tail leaped at it again, but suddenly the frog was gone! It had jumped off the ledge. Stub Tail recklessly sprang after it and landed in a scratchy juniper bush.

As he struggled to push his way out, the hunting cry of the great horned owl boomed through the forest.

*Hoo, hoo, hoo-hoo-hoooo . . .*

The huge bird had been perched near the top of a tall pine where it could watch the forest below. Its quick eyes had not missed what was happening at the bobcat ledge. The owl would not have dared attack a kitten when its mother was near, but now here was a fat little cat alone with a frog at the foot of the ledge. The owl called again as it floated softly down out of the pine.

Stub Tail had pounced on the frog, but when that dreaded hunting cry sounded close above him, he became stiff with fright. The owl's noiseless wings spread over him, shutting out the stars. Flaming eyes stared down, a sharp beak snapped. Then suddenly Stub Tail was grabbed by the back of his neck. His mother had heard the owl's cry and had arrived just in time to swing Stub Tail out of the way. The owl's talons sank into the frog instead.

Great wings flapped skyward. The mother bobcat dropped her kitten and flung herself at the owl. She reared on her hind legs and furiously swung a paw, but only a few feathers floated down.

*Yeow-ow-owwwww!* The mother cat screamed as she watched the owl fly away with the frog.

Stub Tail crowded as close to his mother as he could get.

She picked him up by the back of his neck and lugged him back to the ledge, where she dropped him beside his trembling sister. Then, just to relieve her feelings, she pinned the two of them down with her paw and gave them the scrubbing of their lives.

That evening's adventure had taught Stub Tail and his sister that terrible danger could come from the sky. But there had been something thrilling about Stub Tail's scuffle with the live frog. It was the beginning of his life as a hunter.

# 3. Woodland Neighbors

NEAR DUSK on a June day, the mother bobcat led her kittens on their first walk away from the den. Stub Tail and his sister were now two months old. For several weeks they had been eating the game that their mother brought home. Now it was time for them to learn to hunt for themselves.

The mother cat padded through the woods with the kittens close behind her. Instinct warned the young ones that this was no time for play. When their mother crossed the narrow wood road at the foot of Juniper Hill, they moved behind her as softly as little ghosts. At the edge of the old Indian field, the family paused in a thicket of birch trees. Shadows had gathered in the woods, but the rose and lilac colors of sunset still lingered in the sky. Stub Tail's mother carefully studied the field before moving out into the open. Stub Tail and his sister copied everything she did, so now they too looked about with bright, inquiring eyes.

Two deer, drinking at the edge of the pond, flung up their

heads in alarm as the breeze brought them the scent of bobcat. A moment later they were fleeing in great bounds across the field and into the forest. Stub Tail's mother let them go without a quiver of her whiskers. Venison was good food, but unless she and her kittens were extremely hungry, she would not attack an animal as large as a deer. Tonight she was after small game which the kittens would be able to handle for themselves.

Out in the field, the grass swayed as something moved about in its depths. The mother cat flattened out with her belly to the ground and stole into the grass. The kittens crawled after her.

Up ahead, there were squeals and squeaks and scurrying sounds, as fat little meadow mice came out of their burrows to play in the twilight. Stub Tail's mother paused, and then gave a great bound. She came down with a mouse under each front paw.

The other mice scattered in panic. Stub Tail tried to catch one, but it disappeared into a hole. He sniffed hungrily around the hole and tried to put his paw inside it, but it was too small. He returned to where his mother and sister were eating the mice his mother had caught. When he approached, his sister hastily swallowed the last bite of hers.

Their mother was moving through the grass toward the pond, with the kittens strung out behind her. Stub Tail was

curious about everything he saw or smelled. He stopped to
sniff at a big beetle and turn it over with his paw. A low cry
from his mother sent him hurrying after her, with the beetle
dangling from his mouth. He stopped to crush it with his
teeth, but it did little to satisfy his hunger.

By the time they reached the bank of the pond, the sunset
colors had faded and the reflections of stars were twinkling
in the quiet water. Stub Tail stared at the water in wonder.
There were many new things here for a young bobcat to see,
and hear, and smell!

Not far from shore, a big fish jumped to catch a moth that had been flying low over the water. The head of a swimming mink made a V-shaped ripple. At the edge of the beach a frog began to croak. Stub Tail's ears pricked up. The frog his mother had brought to the ledge made a sound like that. He stole out on the rocky beach.

He could see the frog squatting in the shallow water. It was not as large as the one that the owl had carried off. Stub Tail made a flying leap with paws stretched wide and claws out, as he had seen his mother do. He landed on top of the

slippery frog. It tried to slide away, but he held it fast with teeth and claws. He bit its neck. A second bite killed it.

Stub Tail splashed ashore with the frog in his jaws. His feet were wet but he didn't care. He laid the frog down and began to eat it, crunching up bones and all.

The moon had risen above the trees on Juniper Hill to shed
its magical silvery light on the field and the pond. Suddenly
the beach was alive with little hoptoads. Sight of the leaping
toads drove the kittens wild and they ran here and there, and
even managed to catch a toad or two. But when their mother
called them with a low, sharp cry, they returned to her
immediately.

The mother cat was gazing alertly at another woodland
family that had come softly across the field from the dark

31

forest. It was a mother raccoon and her three furry cubs. In the bright moonlight, the black masks on their faces stood out boldly. The mother raccoon stopped and stared at Stub Tail's mother.

Stub Tail took a few steps forward and a chubby little raccoon came to meet him.

*Meow.*

It was Stub Tail's way of saying that he wanted to play. The little raccoon answered with a soft, chirring sound. Stub Tail thrust out his head and they touched noses. But before they could begin a game, each little one was called by his mother, and the youngsters obeyed at once.

Stub Tail's mother started across the field toward a place where she knew a woodchuck had his burrow. Back on the beach, the mother raccoon was showing her cubs how to dig for mussels in the shallow water near some rocks.

After that first walk to the pond, the bobcat family did not return to the den on the ledge. After a hearty supper of woodchuck, they curled up contentedly to sleep in a hollow near the foot of Juniper Hill.

They would wander freely through the mother cat's hunting territory. Sometimes they would find a place to sleep under the drooping branches of a spruce tree, or against an old log. In rainy weather, they would find a cozy napping place beneath a vine-covered deadfall of trees. Most often they hunted by night, when their marvelous eyesight made it easy for them to see their prey.

During these weeks of summer, the little bobcats watched their mother at her hunting, and in this way they learned to be skilled hunters themselves. But they always stayed close to her, because they were still too small to protect themselves against foxes and other hungry predators.

# 4. Another Kind of Neighbor

IT WAS EARLY on a clear morning in August; the sun was just peeking over the tops of the pines on Juniper Hill. The woods were cool and fresh with morning scents of ferns, and moss, and pine needles. The bobcat family was asleep under a hemlock tree.

Stub Tail was awakened by a tapping on the tree trunk. He looked up through the green branches to where a red-breasted nuthatch was using its sharp beak to dig insects out of the bark. While Stub Tail watched, the little bird crept down the tree to try another place. Suddenly it noticed the three cats on the ground below. It gave a tiny cry of alarm and flew away.

In trees all around, chickadees were talking to one another with cheery humming songs. Stub Tail turned lazily on his back and lay sprawled with all four paws in the air. He felt good. On last night's hunt, he had lain in wait beside a rabbit runway and killed a young cottontail when it came along.

High up in the hemlock, a red squirrel awoke in his bed in the crotch of a branch. He sat up and scratched behind his ear, and then greeted the morning with a burst of noisy chatter. His bright beady eyes quested here and there, taking in everything in the woodland about him. When he spotted the bobcats, his bushy tail jerked with delight. Here were creatures he could tease without any danger to himself! He knew that bobcats were too slow and heavy in trees to catch him if he had to run away. He pulled off a hemlock cone and let it drop.

Plop! The cone hit Stub Tail's furry belly. A second cone fell on his nose. Stub Tail jumped to his feet and peered up through the branches. Saucy chatter from above told him who his tormentor was. He had been teased by squirrels many times before. He gave an angry yowl and started to claw his way up the tree. The squirrel frisked around the trunk and threw down more cones. One hit Stub Tail in the eye. With a mocking bark the squirrel raced away through the branches. Stub Tail knew when he was licked. Growling, he backed down the tree.

He was wide awake now and feeling cross. The squirrel's chatter had awakened his sister. She reached out a paw to bat playfully at Stub Tail, but he growled and turned away.

Suddenly he remembered a patch of catnip he had found near the pond. A longing for the plant's minty fragrance and taste came over him and he padded away through the woods.

Just as Stub Tail was crossing the road at the foot of the hill, something jumped on him from behind. A playful snarl told him that it was his sister. He tried to shake her off, but she clung to him with teeth and claws. Stub Tail went down and they rolled about in the narrow road, pawing and biting. They were so taken up with their rough play that they were unaware of the boy who came around a bend in the road.

The boy stopped short and stared at the bobcats in astonishment and delight. He lived on the farm at the lower end of the pond, and although he knew that there were bobcats in the woods, he had never seen one before.

Stub Tail suddenly realized that a strange two-legged creature was standing in the road. He sprang to his feet, and with a startled glance at the boy, scampered into the woods with his sister close behind him.

The boy drew a deep breath as he stared after the fleeing kittens. It was one of the most exciting moments of his life, but he decided not to mention it to his father and older brother. They were farmers and they regarded all wild predators as a menace to their stock. Word that bobcats were living on Juniper Hill would be sure to bring them out with their guns and dogs.

Back in the woods, Stub Tail and his sister separated. The little female ran back to her mother. Stub Tail sneaked back to the road. Like all cats, he was curious, especially about anything that was new or strange. He wanted a better look at that odd, two-legged creature.

When he reached the pond, there the creature was, standing on a point of land that thrust out into the water! Stub Tail crept as close as he dared. Crouched down behind a clump of daisies, he watched the boy cast a long line out into the water. A few minutes later, he reeled the line in, and there, splashing and leaping at the end, was a good-sized fish! The boy landed the fish on the beach, where it flopped about and almost drove Stub Tail mad with excitement, until the boy killed it with a blow on the head. Stub Tail was so interested that he forgot to be careful. The grass above him swayed as he crept closer to the fish.

Out of the corner of his eye, the boy saw the movement and knew that some animal was there. He turned his head cautiously, and a grin crossed his face when he saw two tufted ears sticking up above the grass. Bobcat ears! Quickly he turned back to his fishing, but he stood so that he could watch that pair of ears.

In his hiding place, Stub Tail was quivering with eagerness. All his instinct and his training warned him that he should go no closer to the creature on the point, but he was hungry for that fat fish! He waited until the boy seemed to be looking

the other way, then bounded recklessly out on the beach. He sank his teeth into the fish and started to drag it into the grass.

Suddenly the boy gave a wild yell and turned around. Terrified, Stub Tail dropped the fish and streaked away, belly to the ground and ears laid flat. He tore across the road and into the woods, where he flattened out behind a juniper bush. The pink tip of his tongue thrust out of his mouth as he watched anxiously to see whether the strange creature was following him.

The boy looked regretfully toward the place where the kitten had disappeared. It was a mean trick, he thought, to scare the little fellow. Later, when he started home, carrying a stringer that dripped with bass and perch, he left the first fish on the beach. Perhaps the kitten would return and claim it after he was gone.

Stub Tail waited behind the juniper until the boy was out of sight down the road. Then he did indeed steal back to the beach. The fish was still there! He pounced on it hungrily and it soon disappeared, bones and all.

After that, Stub Tail sometimes saw the boy again, when he came to fish, or to hunt for arrowheads in the old field. Stub Tail was careful to keep out of sight. Quite often he found a fish on the beach, left especially for him.

# 5. The Hunting Season

OCTOBER BROUGHT brisk cool days and frosty nights. The scarlet and flame of maple trees and the shimmering gold of white birches made bright patches in the evergreen forest. The bobcats' coats grew heavier, with a thick, soft undercoat of fur, which would keep them warm in the icy days to come.

Stub Tail and his sister were half-grown and almost as large as their mother. Their legs were sturdy and powerful. The dark spots on their rust-brown coats had faded. Now they were marked with cloudy blotches and bars, which blended with the light and shadow of the forest, making it easy for them to hide when they were stalking prey. Their underparts were creamy white with faint markings. Their baby teeth had grown and sharpened into the fearsome fangs of predators, but their faces, with their delicate sweeping whiskers and jaunty ear tufts, were still round and beautiful—except when they were angry.

The young bobcats had become skilled hunters and were

now able to feed themselves, but they stayed with their mother as the autumn days passed.

One evening Stub Tail awoke. He had been sleeping with his back against a big log. His mother and sister were still asleep. He stretched and yawned, then vigorously sharpened his claws on the log. Hunting had been poor the night before and he was hungry. He walked softly down through the woods to the old Indian field.

A full moon was sailing in the cloud-swept sky, shedding its silvery light on forest, field, and pond. In the field, the cottontail rabbits had left their burrows to feed on the tender bark of young birch trees. The spicy taste of the birch and the magical light of the moon combined to put them in a carefree, playful mood, and they began to hop and leap about in a rabbit dance. Their long ears waved, and their cotton fluffs of tails twinkled in the moonlight.

Stub Tail crept toward them through the frosted grass. He was almost within leaping distance when the wind changed and carried his pungent cat odor to the cottontails. In a flash the rabbits separated and fled in panic.

Stub Tail could run very fast for a short distance. He took off after the largest rabbit, and he was close upon it when a powerful, huge bobcat sprang out of a clump of young pines and seized the rabbit in his jaws. Stub Tail stopped so suddenly that his paws skidded and he almost sat down.

One bite had killed the rabbit. The big bobcat laid it on

the ground and stood over it. His blazing eyes challenged Stub Tail to come on. Stub Tail snarled in fury. The strange cat was much bigger than he—but had stolen his rabbit! He crept closer to the stranger. He was working himself up to attack when he heard a familiar warning cry.

Stub Tail's mother had come striding across the field, followed by his sister. The mother bobcat went close to the stranger and rubbed her head against his shoulder. A deep hoarse purring came from the big cat. Stub Tail's mother was purring too.

The stranger was Stub Tail's father. He had come back from his own hunting territory to stay with his family over the winter. Soon the young ones accepted him, but they were never friendly or playful with him, as they were with their mother.

Hunting was not as good as it had been during the summer. After the first hard frosts, frogs no longer haunted the pond shore. More and more, chipmunks and woodchucks stayed deep in their warm burrows. With bobcats, foxes, and weasels hunting them more fiercely, rabbits were becoming scarce. And now the deer-hunting season had arrived.

Red-capped hunters seemed to be everywhere in the woods. The bobcats moved cautiously from one hiding place to another, and usually they hunted only at night. But one day, near sunrise, Stub Tail lingered in the field after the others

had sought a safe sleeping place. Hunting that night had brought only two rabbits to share among four bobcats, and Stub Tail was still hungry. He prowled about the field and managed to catch a partridge that was huddled among the birch trees. Its wing had been broken by a bullet and it could not fly away. Stub Tail ate it and licked his whiskers with pleasure.

The sun was rising now, and the eastern sky was aglow with rosy fire. A burst of gunfire in the woods warned Stub Tail that there were hunters about—it was time he found a hiding place. Just as he was crossing the wood road, a hunter walked around a bend. At the sight of a bobcat the man flung up his gun and fired a quick shot. The crack of the rifle, the zing of the bullet, and pain like fire where the bullet creased his back sent Stub Tail streaking up through the woods in terror.

He sought his favorite hiding place under the drooping branches of an old spruce tree. There he squirmed about until he could lick his wound, and after awhile he fell asleep. He stayed hidden all that day and the following night. Then thirst drove him down to the pond. His wound was healing, but he would never forget the pain of it, or the sound of the gun. After that, the sight of a human being would always mean pain and terror to him.

The hunting season closed, the hunters disappeared from the woods, and the bobcats felt once more that the woodland belonged to them. But often they went hungry because of the scarcity of rabbits. One night they happened on a deer shivering in a thicket of hemlocks. It tried to run from them, but it had only three legs and it was weak from loss of blood. One of its legs had been shattered by a bullet and it had been dragging about, slowly dying. It collapsed and Stub Tail's mother sprang at its throat and killed it.

The bobcat family enjoyed a rare feast of venison. When they had eaten all they could, they clawed leaves and needles over the rest of the meat to hide it from other predators.

They stayed nearby until the last scrap of venison was gone. Then they went on their way, leaving the bones and antlers for wood mice to gnaw.

# 6. A Daring Raid

THE LILAC HAZE of Indian summer hung over the hills. In the golden warmth of the sun, all nature seemed to be dreaming of summer days gone by, but night brought heavier frosts, and then came the first snow flurries. Snow was a new experience for Stub Tail. When he first walked in it, he kept lifting his paws and shaking them in disgust. By the time he became used to the cold wet stuff, the first snow had disappeared.

On the farm at the foot of the pond, the chickens were still out on the fenced range where they lived in summer. Stub Tail's father was very much interested in those chickens. Often he would sit on a wooded knoll that overlooked the range, and his eyes would blaze hungrily as he watched the plump hens clucking and scratching. Although his family followed him to the knoll, his mate was uneasy about venturing so close to man and his animals. She hid herself in the branches of a

# 7. Stub Tail on His Own

HOWLING WINTER winds tore the last tattered leaves off the hardwood trees. The evergreens loomed a darker green than they had been in summer, and their branches glittered with a dusting of snow. A white frosting of snow covered the ground in woodland and field, crisscrossed by the tracks of many animals.

Since the death of the father bobcat, the other members of the little family had become more and more independent of one another. Stub Tail and his sister no longer needed their mother for protection and food, and she was now almost indifferent to them. Soon now, some male bobcat, wandering in search of a mate, would happen by. And in the spring, there would be a new family of bobcats in the den on Juniper Hill.

One night Stub Tail's sister went hunting by herself. Two days passed and she did not return. She had found the hunting good in the woods near the farm, and she went there often.

On this night she came upon a snowshoe trail, which had been made by the oldest boy at the farm when he set out a trapline in the woods. The young female followed the curious trail, and before long she came upon a chunk of meat lying under a bush. Here was easy hunting indeed! She pounced on the bait, and as she came down, there was a vicious snap and a trap closed on a front paw. All night in pain and fury she fought to free herself. The following day, a shot rang out in the woods and the boy carried home a dead bobcat to add to his catch of furs. He was pleased, for the soft fur of bobcats was fashionable and costly in the fur market.

Stub Tail never knew what had happened to his sister, and after a few days he did not miss her. He himself stayed well away from the woods near the farm. But one night, when he happened on a snowshoe trail on the wood road, he stopped and sniffed at it out of curiosity, for he had never seen such tracks before. When he caught the whiff of man scent in the track, he backed off and bounded up through the woods. The snowshoe trail had been made by the younger farm boy, out for a harmless walk in the winter woods, but now to Stub Tail any human being was dangerous.

That night he crossed over Juniper Hill and came down in the valley beyond. This was new country to him. He crouched in some bushes beside a well-traveled road and watched in terror as an automobile sped by. He heard dogs barking in the distance. This was no place for a bobcat! He streaked across the road, into the woods, and kept going until he climbed a densely wooded ridge.

On the other side of the ridge, Stub Tail found a wilderness valley, watered by a stream that was frozen now under a glittering roof of ice. In past years a forest fire had swept through this valley and destroyed most of the great, century-old trees. Since then, a lush new growth of birch trees, alders, berry bushes, and bushy young pines and firs had sprung up. Stub Tail began a cautious exploration of the valley. Prowling along the bank of the frozen stream, he came to a pond and a beaver dam and lodge, surrounded by a meadow.

Beavers were new to Stub Tail. He strode out on the ice and sniffed at the snow-covered lodge. The strong scent of beaver came up through an air hole. Stub Tail gave a hungry *meower-ow* and clawed at the rough sticks that formed the lodge, but they were cemented strongly together by beaver building skill and winter ice. The beavers were safe inside their lodge with its underwater entrance.

In the meadow, with its clumps of trees scattered here and there, tracks of deer, foxes, and rabbits made a pattern in the snow, but there was not a single bobcat track except those made by Stub Tail's neat, round paws. This wild valley had been the home hunting range of his father, the biggest and strongest cat for many miles around. While the great cat had lived there, no other cat had dared to intrude, and his death was still too recent for others to know that he was gone forever. Now Stub Tail was free to claim the valley as his own.

Back in the woods, he came upon a huge hollow log lying in a thicket of young firs. Tired after his long journey, he crept into the log and found refuge from the wind and cold. The eastern sky was agleam with the silvery light of early morning. Stub Tail curled up contentedly and slept all day.

When he awoke, a pale gold crescent moon hung in the starry sky. Stub Tail crawled out of his log and stretched his legs. Then he leaped up on the log and sharpened his claws.

The cold, clear air gave him a keen appetite, and he started out eagerly to hunt for supper, moving silently as a shadow. At the edge of the meadow he came to a rabbit runway that led through a tangle of young trees. He flattened himself beside it and waited. Soon a rabbit came hopping along and stopped to nibble the bark on a tree, close to where Stub Tail was hiding. Stub Tail pounced and pinned it beneath his paws.

After making a hearty meal, Stub Tail continued to investigate his new home. As he prowled through the meadow and the surrounding woods, he scattered his scent on trees and rocks, and on mounds of snow and leaves that he scratched up. Sometimes, when he came to a good-sized tree that had escaped the fire, he reached up to leave deep claw marks as high as he could on the trunk. No matter how he stretched himself, he could never reach as high as the old scratches left on many trees by his father. But his marks were high enough, and deep enough, to warn any other cat who might happen along that a bobcat who was a big, fierce fellow was claiming this range for his own.

Day by day the sun swung farther north and the daylight hours lengthened. The snow and ice melted and the stream made woodland music as it murmured and sang on its way to the beaver pond.

With the ice gone from the pond, the beavers set busily to work to repair the damage that winter had done to their

dam. Stub Tail would hide nearby and watch them with eager curiosity. These fat creatures would surely make rich eating! He tried time and again to catch one when they swam ashore to feed, or to cut down a tree with their sharp, chisel teeth. But the beavers were, perhaps, the most cautious animals in the wilderness. There was always one standing watch, and if a predator appeared, or was scented, slap would go the sentry's flat tail on the pond surface. And later in the spring, when the chubby little beaver kits came on shore to play and make mud pies, a big female was always with them.

Once when Stub Tail rushed at one of the kits, an old female turned on him with her big yellow teeth bared in a snarl. Stub Tail rocked back on his paws in astonishment. Before he recovered himself, the kits and their nurse had all disappeared beneath the surface of the pond. Stub Tail yowled in disappointment. But all during that spring he never stopped trying to catch a beaver.

# 8. Stub Tail Defends His Range

ALTHOUGH HE never did succeed in catching one of the wary beavers, Stub Tail found good hunting in his new domain. He could always make a meal of two or three plump mice, and sometimes he surprised a muskrat along the pond shore. There were cottontails, and after a fight with a woodchuck, he added that chunky animal to his menu—at the cost of several painful bites.

One morning in spring, a sound like the rolling of a drum sounded through the woods near the beaver pond. Stub Tail had heard that sound before, on Juniper Hill, and he knew that the drumming was connected with good eating. He crept through the forest and hid himself under a fringe of hemlock branches at the edge of a little glade. Peering out eagerly, he saw a big cock partridge perched on a log.

The partridge was making the drumming sound by vigorously fanning his wings. A shy, plump hen partridge was watching him admiringly from a clump of ferns. The cock stopped drumming and commenced strutting up and down on the log with his ruff spread wide and his beautiful tail opened to a fan. Stub Tail was unable to contain himself any longer. He shot out of his hiding place and leaped upon the log with paws spread wide and claws extended. But even in the ardor of his courting display, the partridge had been on the alert for danger. His strong wings seemed to explode in Stub Tail's face, and he sped away before a paw had touched him. With a thunder of wings, the hen took off also and disappeared among the trees.

Stub Tail padded grumpily on his way through the woodland to where a fallen tree made a bridge across the stream. He was about to cross the tree bridge when a movement in the trees on the other side of the stream caught his eye. A moment later a big black bear came into view, followed by two fat, rollicking cubs. They, too, were headed toward the bridge. Suddenly the mother bear caught the scent of bobcat. She paused and stood on her hind legs to stare about suspiciously—but Stub Tail was no longer there! He was racing upstream and he did not stop until he had put a safe distance between himself and the bear family.

He wandered here and there in his valley, stopping often to investigate a thicket or to peer into some crevice in the rocks. In a marshy place he met a painted turtle, crawling toward higher ground to lay her eggs. The turtle immediately pulled in her head and shut herself inside the fortress of her shell. Stub Tail pawed at the shell and shoved it about, but finally he gave up trying to open it and went on his way.

His attention was soon captured by the flash of golden wings, and he turned his head in time to see a flicker disappear into a hole high in a tree trunk. Certain that the hole contained the flicker's nest and nestlings, Stub Tail hungrily started to claw his way up the tree trunk. He was only halfway to the hole when one flicker shot out of it and a second one arrowed down at him from a high branch. The pair flew recklessly around his head, uttering angry cries, beating at him with their wings, and pecking at him with their strong beaks. A pair of bluejays that had a nest in a nearby tree flew screaming to join in the attack. Stub Tail almost fell off the tree as he tried to fend off the furious birds with one paw while he held on with the other. Battered, and almost in a panic, he backed to the ground and left with as much dignity as he could muster. The birds followed him a short distance, screaming and squawking, but finally they turned back to their nests and left him in peace.

Stub Tail was now feeling very much out of sorts. He had been put to flight by a bear, successfully resisted by a turtle, and defeated in a battle with birds! He sat down and washed himself thoroughly.

Suddenly his attention was caught by something on a nearby

tree trunk. Some animal had been scratching the bark of this tree, and it couldn't have been any animal but a bobcat, and a good-sized bobcat at that! Stub Tail sniffed around the base of the tree. He snarled, and his claws worked angrily in and out of his paws when he discovered that the strange cat had dared to mark the tree—his, Stub Tail's tree—with his scent. He stood on his hind legs and reached high to make claw marks of his own. His reach was a little higher than that of the strange cat, but the stranger's claw marks were deep and strong.

Growling in his throat, Stub Tail set out to find the bold invader of his territory.

The trail was quite fresh and easy to follow. Here he found a fresh paw track in the moist earth. There he came upon the remains of a rabbit, killed and eaten only a short time before. Stub Tail showed his fangs in a snarl, his ears flattened, and his face became a mask of fury. But he did not forget caution

as he stole in and out of the forest shadows, watching and listening for the stranger cat.

The woodland had become hushed in a sort of enchanted stillness. Not a birdsong sounded in the trees, not a single mouse or chipmunk scurried through the mosses, ferns, and dry leaves. Even the squirrels were quiet.

Stub Tail found more claw marks and scent signs. He investigated each one and then went on until he saw, looming ahead, a huge boulder overgrown with moss and little ferns. He stopped to study it carefully. Suddenly the fur on the back of his neck prickled and lifted as some inner sense warned him of danger. He leaped to one side and whirled about just in time to see another bobcat jump from the rock to the ground where Stub Tail had been only a moment before.

Stub Tail crouched low. The stranger faced him boldly, a fine, strong cat, as large as Stub Tail himself. His eyes glittered with hate. His long fangs gleamed in his open mouth.

*Yow-yow-yowerrr-ow!* he screamed in challenge.

Stub Tail's voice rose in an answering shriek. *Meowerr-ow-yow-yowww!*

The two big cats approached each other slowly and circled, stiff-legged and menacing. When they were within striking distance, they paused to make hideous screeches, yowls, and caterwauls, each cat trying to frighten the other. Their short tails were whipping angrily, and the fur stood up all over their bodies, making them look twice as large as they really were. Then suddenly Stub Tail flung himself on the stranger and fastened his teeth in his ear. The stranger jerked away, leaving a piece of his ear in Stub Tail's teeth. They came together again in a pinwheel and fell to the ground, spitting, snarling, clawing, and biting. Fur flew as they rolled about. The stranger was getting the worst of it and he knew it. He fought himself free and bounded away. Stub Tail pursued him for only a short distance. He knew that the defeated cat would not return.

Except for a few painful scratches and a bitten paw, Stub Tail was not badly hurt. He walked over to a tree and stood on his toes to stretch himself as tall as possible. His claws dug deep into the bark and worked downward with a tearing

sound. The claw marks began higher than any he had ever made before. It almost seemed that he had grown during the fight.

He scratched vigorously for a few moments, then dropped to all fours. He was tired after the fight, but his spirit was high and his tufted ears stood up proudly. He sat down and carefully licked his wounded paw, and afterward, washed himself all over until his fur gleamed. Then, limping on his hurt paw, he started back through the valley, which was truly his own now, to the comfortable hollow log.